S0-AHC-085

LIGHTNING BOLT BOOKS™

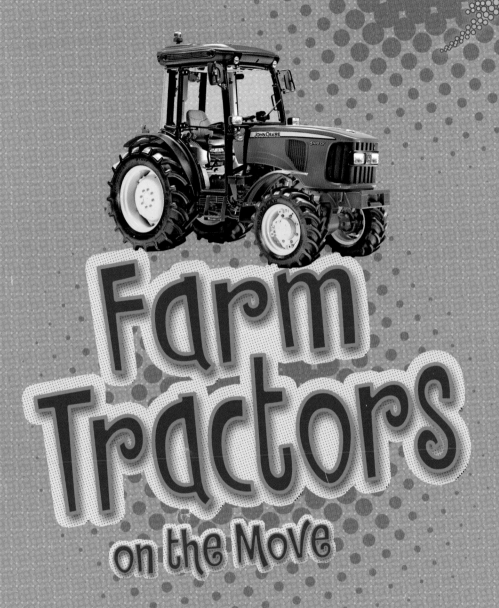

Farm Tractors
on the Move

Kristin L. Nelson

Lerner Publications Company
Minneapolis

Lerner Publications Company
A division of Lerner Publishing Group, Inc.
241 First Avenue North
Minneapolis, MN 55401 U.S.A.

Website address: www.lernerbooks.com

Library of Congress Cataloging-in-Publication Data

Nelson, Kristin L.
    Farm tractors on the move / by Kristin L. Nelson.
        p.   cm. — (Lightning bolt books ™ — Vroom-vroom)
    Includes index.
    ISBN 978–0–7613–6025–4 (lib. bdg. : alk. paper)
    1. Farm tractors—Juvenile literature. 2. Farms—Juvenile literature. I. Title.
 S711.N383 2011
 631.3′72—dc22   2010018169

Manufactured in the United States of America
1 — CG — 12/31/10

Contents

Farm Tractors

What kind of machine has big, bumpy tires like this one?

Farm tractors!

The bumps help tractors drive over rocky ground and mud without slipping.

This tractor has no trouble driving over a bumpy field.

Tractors spend most
days in the dirt.
They help farmers do
many jobs.

Tractor Parts

A farmer controls a tractor with a steering wheel. The steering wheel makes a tractor turn.

A grandfather shows his grandson how this tractor's steering wheel works.

This farmer sits in a cab to steer his tractor. A cab has windows on the front and on each side.

In front of the cab are small, round parts that help farmers see in the dark. **Can you name them?**

What is this part of the tractor called?

They are headlights.

They make light so
farmers can work at night.

A tractor has another part that helps farmers work. On the back of a tractor is a hitch. A hitch hooks up the tractor to machines that do many jobs.

This hitch hooks up the tractor to a plow.

Planting

Some machines ready the ground for planting. This tractor pulls a plow. The plow's blades dig into the dirt. Then they turn it over.

Plowed dirt is lumpy.

The tractor pulls a harrow. This machine's round blades cut through the lumps.

Next, the farmer hitches a
seed drill to the tractor.
A seed drill's blades make
holes in the dirt.

Seed drills help
farmers plant crops.

Then the drill drops seeds
into the holes. It covers
them with dirt.

What happens to seeds
after they are planted?

Sun and rain
help seeds grow.
They turn into
corn and other
crops!

Corn grows
on a stalk.

Harvesting

A tractor works with a combine to cut and gather this corn. This is called harvesting.

These string beans are
harvested by a tractor that
pulls a bean picker.
The picker has
skinny metal
fingers that
gather the beans.

Workers pack the string beans into boxes. The beans are ready to go to the grocery store.

Do you like to eat string beans?

Here is another harvesting job.

This tractor pulls a mower to cut grass.

Next, a giant rake turns
over the cut grass. The grass
dries quickly in the sun.
It becomes hay.

The tractor tows a baler through the field. A baler collects the hay and rolls it into bales.

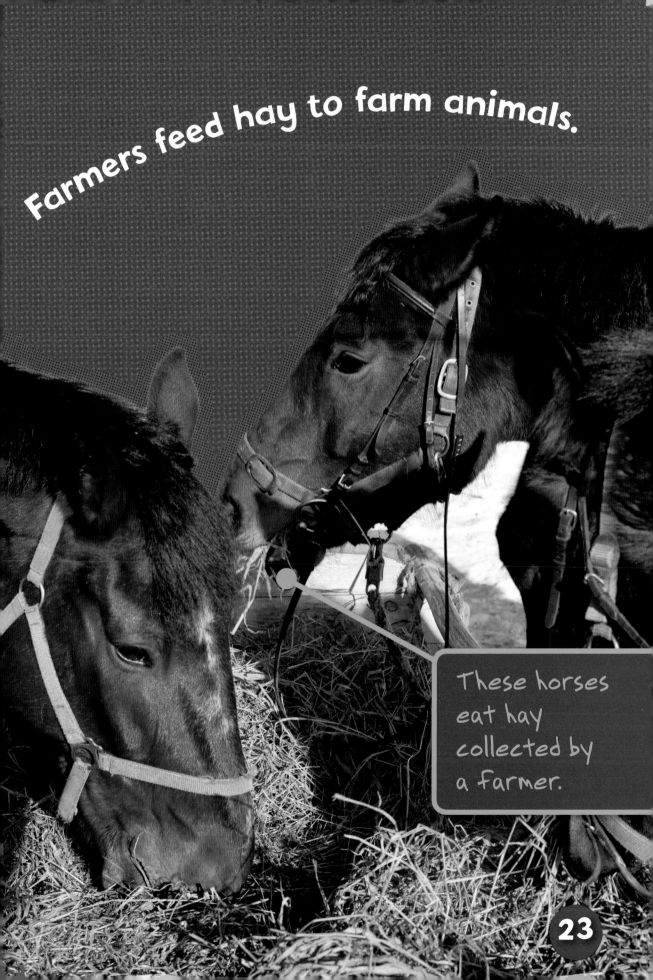

Farmers feed hay to farm animals.

These horses eat hay collected by a farmer.

More Tractor Jobs

Tractors have other jobs too. This tractor uses a big shovel to clean up the barn.

**This tractor cuts a lawn.
Can tractors be used
for fun too?**

Yes!
This tractor is taking children for a ride on a trailer.

Children ride on a trailer with their parents through a pumpkin patch.

Tractors plant seeds and harvest crops. Tractors pull plows and trailers. Tractors are very useful.

Farm Tractor Diagram

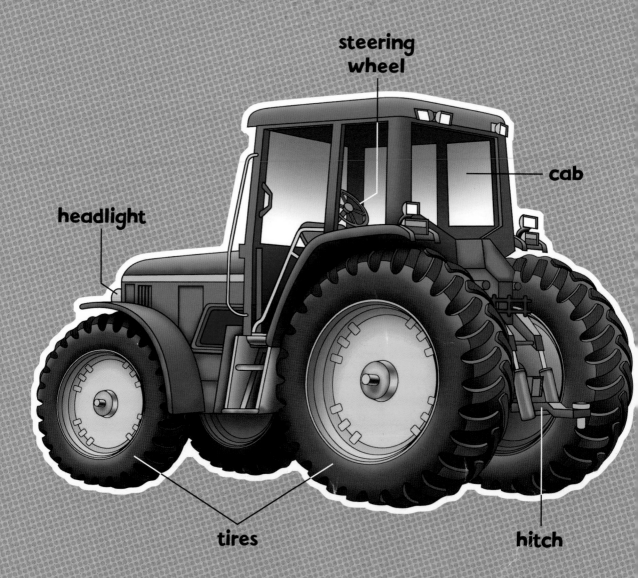

steering wheel

cab

headlight

tires

hitch

Fun Facts

- Farm tractors do jobs besides the ones shown in this book. They can pull machines that chop weeds. They can stack bales of hay. They can spray crops to keep bugs away.

- A farm tractor gets its power from an engine. Before engines were invented, horses pulled most farm machines.

- Some people collect old tractors for fun. An old, rare tractor can be worth thousands of dollars!

- Another fun hobby is tractor pulling. Pullers fix up their tractors to be powerful. Then they have a contest to see which tractor can pull a heavy weight the farthest.

Glossary

cab: the part of a tractor where the driver sits. A cab has windows on its front and on each side.

harvesting: collecting crops from a field

headlight: a light on the front of a tractor

hitch: a hook on the back of a tractor that connects it to farm machines

steering wheel: a round tractor part that turns the tractor's wheels

Further Reading

Alexander, Heather. *Big Book of Tractors.* New York: Parachute Press: DK, 2007.

Brecke, Nicole, and Patricia M. Stockland. *Cars, Trucks and Motorcycles You Can Draw.* Minneapolis: Millbrook Press, 2010.

Enchanted Learning: Vehicle Online Coloring Pages
http://www.enchantedlearning.com/vehicles/paintonline.shtml

FSA Kids
http://www.fsa.usda.gov/FSA/kidsapp?area=home&subject=landing&topic=landing

John Deere Kids' Corner
http://www.deere.com/en_US/compinfo/kidscorner/home.html

Lindeen, Mary. *Tractors.* Minneapolis: Bellwether Media, 2007.

Index

Photo Acknowledgments

The images in this book are used with the permission of: Courtesy John Deere & Company, pp. 1, 6, 8, 10, 17, 25, 29; © Enruta/Dreamstime.com, p. 2; © Hixson/ Dreamstime.com, p. 4; © PhotoStock-Israel/Alamy, p. 5; © Image Source/Getty Images, p. 7; © Grant Heilman Photography/Alamy, pp. 9, 18; © Lomonadv/Dreamstime.com, p. 11; © AGStockUSA/Alamy, p. 12; © Jim Sincock/Dreamstime.com, p. 13; © Monkey Business Images/Dreamstime.com, pp. 14, 15; © Nathan Allred/Dreamstime.com, p. 16; © IndexStock/SuperStock, p. 19; © Robert Read/Alamy, pp. 20, 21; © iStockphoto.com/ Cameron Pashak, p. 22; © Topdeq/Dreamstime.com, p. 23; © David Lorenz Winston, p. 24; © Dennis MacDonald/Alamy, p. 26; © Elena Elisseeva/Dreamstime.com, p. 27; © Laura Westlund/Independent Picture Service, p. 28; © Dary423/Dreamstime.com, p. 30; © Soleg1974/Dreamstime.com, p. 31.

Front cover: © Roman Milert/Dreamstime.com (top); © Duncan Hale-Sutton/ Alamy (bottom).